TOWER POWER

SCHOLASTIC

Conceived and produced by Weldon Owen Pty Ltd,
Ground Floor 42–44 Victoria Street, McMahons Point,
Sydney, NSW 2060, Australia

International Sales Office: kristiner@weldonowen.com.au

Library of Congress Cataloging-in-Publication Data

Evans, Lynette

  Tower power / by Lynette Evans

ISBN 13: 978-0-545-43690-8
ISBN 10: 0-545-43690-7

A CIP catalog record for this book is available from the
Library of Congress.

Published in the United States by
Scholastic Inc.
557 Broadway
New York, New York 10012
www.scholastic.com

12 13 14 15 16 17 18 19
10 9 8 7 6 5 4 3 2 1

Printed by Toppan Leefung in China

The paper used in the manufacture of this book
is sourced from wood grown in sustainable forests.
It complies with the Environmental Management
System Standard ISO 14001:2004

Weldon Owen Pty Ltd
Managing Director Kay Scarlett
Publisher Corinne Roberts
Creative Director Sue Burk

Managing Editors Lynette Evans, Janine Scott
Designer Karen Sagovac
Images Manager Trucie Henderson
Design Assistant Oliver Black
Production Director Todd Rechner
Production and Pre-press Controller Mike Crowton
Production Controller Lisa Conway

Photographs: Corbis 16cl, 16-17c, 18-19c; **Dreamstime**
5tl, 7cr, 20-21c, 22-23c; **Getty Images** 14-15c;
iStockphoto.com front cover c, bg, 1c, 6bc, 3bcr, tc, tcr,
c, 2-3tc, 4-5c, 6br, 8-9c, 9c, 10br, 10-11bg, 12bl, 12-13c,
13cr, 14tl, 15cr, 17cr, 18bl, 18-19bg, 19cr, 20bl, 21tc, 22bl,
tl, 22-23bc, tc, 25cr; **Library of Congress** 3bc, 4-5bg,
6-7bg, 24-25bg; **Shutterstock** 24bc, br, 28bc.

All other photographs and illustrations
© Weldon Owen Pty Ltd

A WELDON OWEN PRODUCTION

CONTENTS

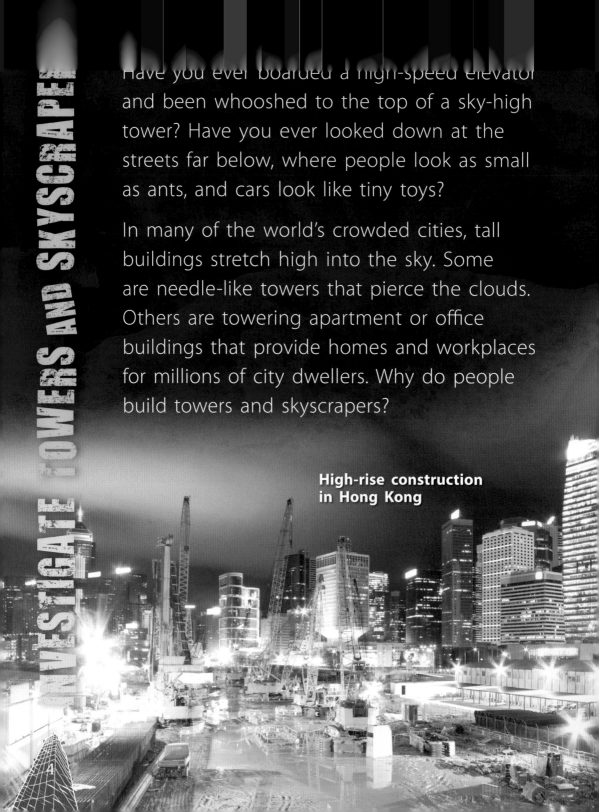

Have you ever boarded a high-speed elevator and been whooshed to the top of a sky-high tower? Have you ever looked down at the streets far below, where people look as small as ants, and cars look like tiny toys?

In many of the world's crowded cities, tall buildings stretch high into the sky. Some are needle-like towers that pierce the clouds. Others are towering apartment or office buildings that provide homes and workplaces for millions of city dwellers. Why do people build towers and skyscrapers?

High-rise construction in Hong Kong

Skyscrapers are useful buildings for crowded cities, where there is little spare land. Skyscrapers provide plenty of vertical space, while taking up little ground space.

Since ancient times, people have built soaring towers, often to show power and wealth. However, the height of early towers was limited by the heavy weight of stone and brick building materials.

It was not until the late 1800s, with the invention of new building materials such as iron, steel, and strong glass, that the construction of skyscrapers really took off – and up, up, UP!

Today, ultra-modern materials, new building methods, and many powerful machines allow people to build higher than ever before.

COMPARE TOWERS, OLD AND NEW

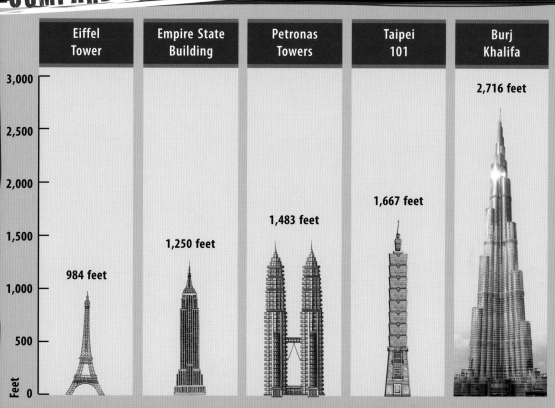

Eiffel Tower	Empire State Building	Petronas Towers	Taipei 101	Burj Khalifa

3,000

2,500

2,000

1,500

1,000

500

0

Feet

984 feet

1,250 feet

1,483 feet

1,667 feet

2,716 feet

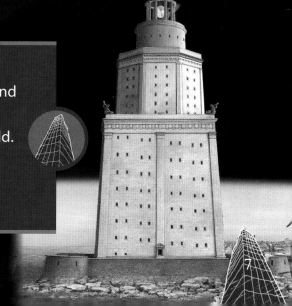

For many hundreds of years, a towering lighthouse on the island of Pharos in Egypt was one of the tallest buildings in the world. It was built in about 290 BCE and was about as tall as the Statue of Liberty.

BUILDING IN THE SAND

Today the world knows this amazing tower as Burj Khalifa, the tallest building in the world. But for six long years, this area was a construction **site**. Before that time, the city of Dubai had a mix of **traditional** and mostly lower-level structures rising here and there from the desert sands.

As the building of the tower began, the city was transformed into a hive of activity, with a swarm of workers buzzing about. Mighty machines lifted and shifted materials as this great, gleaming skyscraper rose high into the blue sky.

Constructing the tallest tower in the world required a talented team of **architects**, **engineers**, builders, and crane operators. At first, the project was a secret. That is, no one seemed to know exactly how high the **megastructure** would be. The only thing they did know was that it was designed to be the tower that would rise above all other towers.

The work began with architects and engineers making extensive models and computer designs. Then it was time to go to the site and oversee the building of the actual structure.

When engineers work with architects, they use mathematical calculations, plans, computer designs, and models to make sure the structures are strong and safe.

VERTICAL CITIES

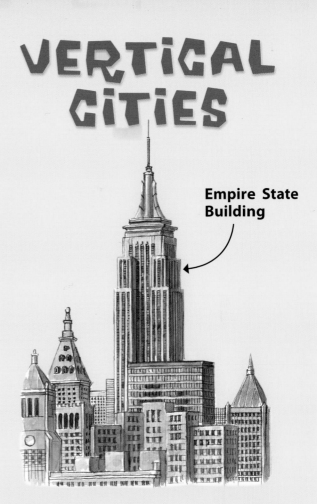

Empire State Building

During the late 1800s, a new and strong building material – steel – became cheaper to produce. In crowded urban areas, people began constructing metal-framed buildings that soared to the skies.

New York City took the lead in skyscraper construction. With its 102 stories, the Empire State Building became the world's tallest building when it was completed in 1931. This world-famous skyscraper is 1,250 feet from sidewalk to roof.

11

On the day they broke ground, mighty diggers rolled in with a roar and a rumble. Over time, the earth was **excavated** so that laying the **foundation** of the superstructure could begin. The foundation was as wide as an entire New York City block!

In the days that followed, concrete trucks began pumping load after load of thick, flowing concrete. As many as 192 concrete **piles** were buried more than 164 feet deep into the ground, and a grid of steel bars helped make the foundation firm.

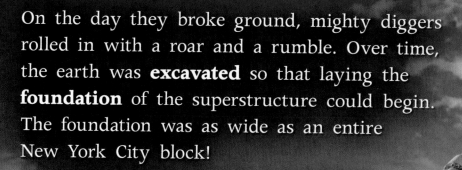

People have used concrete as a building material for thousands of years, but the method of **reinforcing** concrete with strong steel bars was first used in the mid 1800s. This method helped make the construction of super-tall skyscrapers possible.

FiRM FOUNDATiONS

Tall structures need firm foundations to prevent them from toppling over or sinking into the ground. Just like trees are anchored to the ground and supported by their roots, buildings often have long columns made of steel and concrete that go deep below the surface.

Leaning Tower of Pisa

The Leaning Tower of Pisa, in Italy, is famous because of its faulty foundation. Construction began in about 1173, but the tower began to sink after the third floor was added because it was built on unstable soil. Engineers stabilized the tower in the 1990s to keep it from sinking further.

13

Cranes use a system of **pulleys** and attachments, such as hooks and buckets, to lift loads.

More than a year after breaking ground, the building of the tower itself began. A forest of tall cranes swung loads of materials higher and higher as the superstructure inched its way skywards.

The crane operators often worked from dawn till dusk in their mighty machines, lifting and shifting loads of steel and glass. As stories were added, the tower cranes also grew, adding new sections for more height. Then, the powerful pumps started pumping concrete up, up, UP, and the sound of machinery filled the air.

MiGHTY MACHiNES

There are different kinds of cranes. Crawler cranes are mounted on wheels. They have a long arm called a boom.

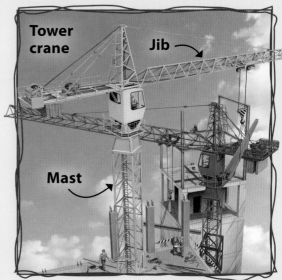

Tower crane
Jib
Mast

Tower cranes are fixed in place. They have a vertical support tower called a mast and a long arm called a jib. The load is on one end of the jib, and a counterbalance is on the other. Sections can be added to the mast to increase the height of a tower crane during construction.

Concrete was pumped higher than concrete had ever been pumped before!

15

As the building stretched higher into the sky, strong winds tugged and blew, but the tower stood firm. Its spiraling steel and concrete core walls helped prevent it from twisting in the wind. Its side wings, or **buttresses**, flared out from the base and tapered upwards to keep the structure stable.

The core of the Burj Khalifa has strong, steel bar, reinforced concrete walls. If all the steel bars were laid end to end, they would stretch more than one quarter of the way around the world!

16

After three long, hard years, the tower reached level 160. The tallest human-made structure on the planet had been built – but the work wasn't finished yet!

MODERN MATERIALS

The invention of iron and steel meant that structures could be higher than ever. The strength of iron was shown to the world in 1889 when Gustave Eiffel had the 984-foot-high Eiffel Tower built in Paris.

Eiffel Tower

Aluminum, stainless steel, and strong glass are modern materials that designers often use for the outside finish, or **cladding**, of skyscrapers today. About 26,000 hand-cut glass panels were used in the cladding of the Burj Khalifa.

17

In the scorching heat of the desert city, work on the great tower continued and the finishing touches were added. A beautiful steel spire was installed at the very top, revealing the secret of the tower's height as a dizzying 2,716 and a half feet!

More than 300 specialists worked to place the cladding on the tower. The cladding, with its aluminum and stainless steel panels, was designed to withstand even the most extreme summer temperatures, and the glass panels were made to reflect the sun's light.

Were the windows self-cleaning? No!

It is a huge task to keep a skyscraper clean and shiny. Experts often use abseiling, or rope climbing, equipment to wash windows high above the ground.

SAFE AND SPEEDY

Skyscrapers have changed the urban landscape since they began to spring up during the 1800s. High-rise buildings became easy to access because of an important invention by Elisha Otis. He demonstrated the world's first safety elevator, fitted with a brake, in 1854.

Glass elevators

Today, high-tech, high-speed elevators zoom up and down the insides and outsides of tall buildings. Some elevators are made of glass, so passengers can have a ride with a view!

19

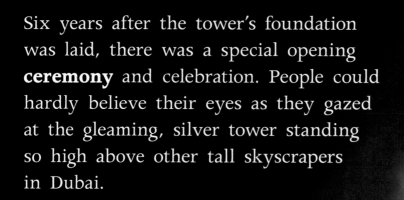

Six years after the tower's foundation was laid, there was a special opening **ceremony** and celebration. People could hardly believe their eyes as they gazed at the gleaming, silver tower standing so high above other tall skyscrapers in Dubai.

As the day ended, the tower was lit, first by the rays of the setting sun, and then by spotlights beaming onto its shiny surface.

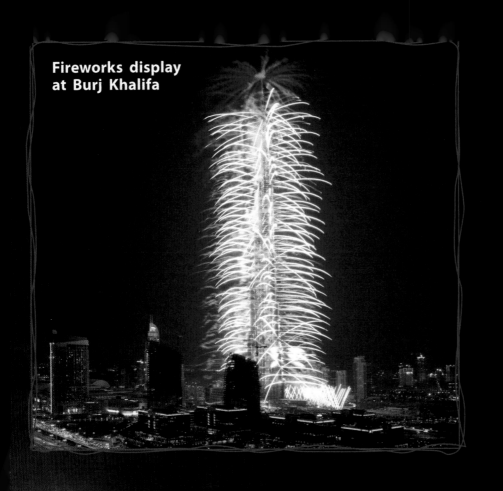

Fireworks display at Burj Khalifa

To complete the celebration of the world's newest, tallest tower, colorful fireworks lit up the night sky!

PETRONAS TOWERS

In 1998, Asia celebrated the completion of the soaring Petronas Towers in Malaysia. These 88-story towers are joined by a skybridge on the 42nd floor. They are 1,483 feet high and for six years were the tallest towers in the world.

EMPIRE STATE BUILDING

When it was built in 1931, the Empire State Building changed the skyline of New York City. At 1,250 feet, it was the world's tallest building for many years.

EIFFEL TOWER

When it was completed in 1889 for the world fair, the Eiffel Tower, in Paris, was the tallest structure ever built. This symbol of France is 984 feet high.

TAIPEI 101

In 2004, a pagoda-like tower in Taiwan, called Taipei 101, became the world's tallest building and stayed so for many years. With 101 stories above ground, it stretches 1,667 feet into the sky.

TALL, TALLER, TALLEST?

Will the tallest ever be tall enough?

BURJ KHALIFA

This almost impossibly tall tower seems to be the pinnacle of high-rise engineering. Completed in 2010 at a height of more than 2,716 feet, it is a record-holder, but for how long?

CONNECT WITH TOWERS

New building materials and methods allow modern towers to be designed in many different shapes and with many incredible finishes. No matter how they look, however, all towers must be tall, strong, and stable. They must stand up to nature's howling winds and rattling earthquakes.

Make a tower out of straws. You will need: drinking straws, sticky tape, scissors, and a measuring tape or a ruler.

1. **Use straws to make a base for the tower.**

2. **To build up, cut a small slit in a straw. Slide another straw into it. Repeat this with the other straws.**

3. **Use sticky tape to hold the straws together. Build the tower as tall as you can without it falling down!**

Predict how high you can build your tower without it falling down. Measure its finished height. Was your prediction correct?

Experiment with different shapes to make your tower stable. Which shapes are strong shapes?

architect – a person who designs structures

buttress – a structure built against a wall to help support it

ceremony – formal words and events to mark an important occasion

cladding – the outside surface or exterior finish of a building

engineer – a person who designs and supervises large construction projects and the building of strong, safe structures

excavate – to dig into the ground and remove earth to put up the supports for a building

foundation – a solid structure, or base, on which a bridge or building is constructed

megastructure – a very large structure

pile – a heavy wood or steel beam that is driven into the ground to support a structure

pulley – a wheel with a grooved rim in which a cable, chain, or rope runs. A pulley is used to lift loads more easily.

reinforce – to strengthen something

site – the place where something is built

traditional – used from one generation to the next

Pyramids and towers are megastructures

Learn the history of skyscrapers all over the world, beginning with the Pyramid of Giza and the Eiffel Tower, and then moving to cities across the globe.

Book

Curlee, Lynn.
Skyscraper
Atheneum Books for Young Readers, 2007.

Web Site

http://www.skyscraper.org/WHAT%27S_UP/COOL_STUFF/coolstuff.htm

Chrysler Building